KT-133-277

Recital

Poems 1975-1980

by

James J. McAuley

THE DOLMEN PRESS

RECITAL is designed by Liam Miller,
printed in the Republic of Ireland
for the publishers, The Dolmen Press,
Mountrath, Portlaoise, Ireland.

Publication of this book was assisted by a grant from An
Comhairle Ealaíon (The Arts Council).

First published 1982

ISBN 0 85105 394 7

© 1982: James J. McAuley

CO. DUBLIN
LIBRARY SERVICE
Acc. No. 053947
Copy... Te 1005
Inv. No. 5476^A
Price... £3·60
Class No. 821 McAul

Copyright under the Berne Convention, all rights reserved. Apart from fair
dealing for study or review, no part of this publication may be reproduced,
stored in a retrieval system, or transmitted, in any form or by any means,
electronic, mechanical, photocopying, recording, or otherwise, without the
prior permission of the Dolmen Press.

for
Anne
Michael
Tish
and their families
with love

ACKNOWLEDGEMENTS

Thanks to the editors of magazines, anthologies, etc., where versions of poems first appeared:

"Ritual", "Losing the Way", "Making an Impression", "Impromptu for Solo Tenor" and "Recital"—*The Irish Press* (New Irish Writing).

"Studies for a Self-Portrait at Forty", "The Exile Considers How His Life is Spent"—*The Malahat Review*.

"Letter to Richard Hugo from Drumcliff" and "Lessons"—CAIM.

"Cheiron" and "Refugees"—*Crazy Horse*.

"The Confession", "An Irish Bull", "The Exile Takes Stock of His Surroundings", "The Exile, *En Famille*" and "Succubus"—*Poetry Northwest*.

"Identikit"—*The Hollins Critic*.

"To His Host, Who Has Asked Him To Stay Longer"—*Red Weather*.

"Timepiece"—*Poetry* (Chicago), October 1978.

"Deposition of Harold Moore, Gardener . . ."—*Cut Bank*.

"Death of Fathers", "Owen at Play", and "The Picture of Little Rory in a Municipal Park"—*Mill Mountain Review*.

"Requiem"—*Black Box* no. 17. Sections IV and VI appeared in *The New Orleans Review*.

"My Ugly Friend" and "Directions"—*Poetry Now*.

"Going Late to Bed"—*Slackwater Review*.

"Lower Case"—*The Greensboro Review*.

"After Yeats, After Ronsard . . ."—*The Irish Times*.

"Take Up Thy Bed"—*The Honest Ulsterman*.

"Natural History"—*Willow Springs*.

"Conclusions"—*The Gorey Detail*.

"For the Three Sons of My First Marriage", and "Drought"—*Kudzu*.

"An Irish Bull" was published by Mill Mountain Press as a Broadside, 1980.

"The Old Writer", "War Criminal", and "The Artist, Reclining" were included in *Iron Country*, ed. F. Alexander, Copper Canyon Press, Port Townsend, Washington, 1979.

"House Burning Down" was selected for the Poets-in-the-Cities Project of Snohomish County (Joan Swift, Director), 1977-78.

"Recital" is included as part of *Praise!*, a theatre piece for orchestra, chorus and tenor soloist, commissioned by the Spokane Symphony Society for performance in February 1981; music composed by Dr. Wendal Jones.

6

CONTENTS

RITUAL

Before I offer the wood,
I whet the knife on a stone
With simple strokes, back and forth,
Thus. I disown these hands,
Empowered by laws that hold
Moon and tide to their pledge.
Steel and stone, flesh and bone,
The blade's light song repeats.
I test its edge on the stony
Heel of my hand before
I offer the tender wood.

I learn again to take pains
With simple things: to take
The knife in my better hand, thus:
And the driftwood, already worn
By the steely waves to a shape
I recognize as if dreamt
While I rocked in those waves myself —
The wood in this hand, so.

The mask of one I recognize
Stares up from the wood. I begin.

9

STUDIES FOR A SELF-PORTRAIT AT FORTY

I

You'd hardly notice at first how everything
Has been arranged in fours—geraniums
In red clusters—and how dark surfaces gleam:
Onyx ashtrays, brass candelabra, the table
Where the white envelopes lie. Tempting, to chop
The thumbs from the hands that ruefully shuffle the letters,
And bury them under the cherry-tree outside,
All brightness, in a cedar cigarette-box
Inlaid with the ivory figure of a woman—
My mother, say, soon after my conception;
Or the nurse who sang while she washed my genitals
When I was feverish. The envelopes
Murmur politely, saying my name four times.

II

Cock the right eyebrow: heredity.
The self-mocker I try to surprise
In the mirror gets a laugh
Out of this repeated peering.

Tempting, to wear the black
Hat with the wide brim, clipped
Moustache, eyes narrowed, cunning.
One self is all art.

III *Episodes for a Panel.*

A whiteskinned boy, halfdrowned,
On a yellow strand, his open
Mouth a black rictus. Later,
He could recall only grey filtered
Light rising over him as he
Sank. Since then, it seemed,

Nothing began or ended: He pushed
Through a dappled, watery
Continuum, as his feet had
Lifted him on the seabed over
The few yards to dry sand.

*

Skinny youth in a garden perspective:
Yews form a nave for statues
Of skinny militant saints.
He kneels at the shrine to the Virgin
Whose marble bosom swells
Through her marble robe.

Flesh oppresses him: rosary
Novenas tremble round his head
In the green eucalyptic air
Like the birds round Saint Francis.

11

*

Plump, shaved, hair cropped, he sits
At the edge of a hospital bed.
A rosy, plump nurse has suffered
His fingers to open her stiff
Uniform, to kiss the perfumed breasts
She consecrates to Jesus
Every morning. Even her smile
Has been trained. He is wide-eyed,
Frowning. This tableau is joyless.

*

Leathery, hirsute, the critic
Stands with didactic tweed
Sleeve raised in a gallery
Of *fin de siècle* portraits
By John Yeats, Lavery, Osborne.

The thoughtful figures converse
With each other, over his head.
In this one too, he is frowning;
Mouth a black ridge, one hand pocketed.

12

IV

Better the big NOW, singular,
No symbolic trappings,
No sad accomplices.
Dante's dark wood at my shoulder?
Or, from his next simile,
Grey seas, a thin wash to signal
Escape from death? Hello, Lazarus.

In this I have my father's features,
With a rime of beard and my mother's eyes.
I look my age. Behind me on every side
Grey seas betray a northfacing
Shore; all painted flat grey
Into the sky it meets
With a darker grey, and mottled
As lichen on stone.

V

Leave the hair white, uncombed.
Change the eyes to suspicious,
Clamp the mouth thin as the line
Marking the horizon
Which in the final version
Will suggest escape from madness.

Open the thin mouth a little,
As if speech went on while the pose
Held long enough for the common
Skull to be implied
Or contained under the skin.

13

When this one hangs in a room,
Ask what the subject asked
While he waited for a shape
Beyond him to be revealed.

Hint at fear and regret
In the pale cheeks, the way
The eyes look at nothing. Now,
It will do; it will have to do.

LETTER TO RICHARD HUGO FROM DRUMCLIFF

Dear Dick, This kind of travel is cheap enough:
Hard a'starboard after a vexing nightmare,
And there I leave you—Mister Yeats at Coole,
Being severe with young poets on Lady Gregory's lawn,
Looking over his specs at a few bedraggled sheep
On the shore of the murky lake. And he counting them swans . . . .

It's just a Byzantine canter through Roscommon,
A fearful county for tinkers, to Drumcliff.
A Philip Larkin chapel, half-buried in old trees;
Bland, tame Gothic of the Established Faith
That none of the neighbours give a damn about,
Keeping to their long-lipped superstitions,
Their guttural gossip making a natural prey
Of the ancestral rector—"He's a nice man, *but* . . . . "
Half-starved mongrels worrying a lame sheep.

The embattled cleric: patrolling his neat grounds,
Pondering his fingernails, the only
Clean set in the parish; preparing to preach mildly
On "Prudence" again, to his congregation of five—
Six, if you counted the deafmute poorhouse orphan,
His only convert, who rang the Communion bell
And pulled the thistles from the gentry's graves.

The peasantry: He sang them plain and cruel,
Dour and quaint; went sour on them, invented
A freckled ghost in tweed with a fly-rod and an ear
Cold enough to hear him out. He caught
Neither salmon nor trout himself; hated low bars;
His women all had double-barrelled names.
How could *we* move in *his* circles? His goddam gyres!

15

Randy laughter, hell! His lightest rhyme
Was strictly Big House—a bronze gong embossed
With gyres, moon-phases, rose, rood, and tower;
Struck well, that great gong calls the lords and ladies
To their places at stage centre, *right*. He warped
The local colours of old saga, older *rann*,
To his own passionate, visionary weft,
As Vergil had for Rome in *her* decline.
Here, beneath white gravel, his immortal, bone-white grin.

There's an old cross at the top of the graveyard lane.
The disproportionate head of the crucified figure
Wears the same dissembling agony-smile.
Some nameless monk, ten centuries ago,
Chipped the lichen off a great rock and cut
Him down to size.
So, that gorgeous gong resounds through Idaho:
Here, the tourist looks up from the arrogant plain stone
To a rook flapping in a galebent oak. It's like
Getting pissed off at Xerxes, as you say. Best, Jim.

CHEIRON

I

When I was a Curragh stableboy,
The filly Amaryllis sank
Her teeth in my shoulder as I bent
To ease her saddlegirth. This killed
In me the romance of these animals.

None of us without our mark from falls
Or rival whips—all of us deathsheads,
Lean as Hindu priests, awkward
As puppets when we walked the ground—
But many who learned nothing from their scars.

No horse I rode could fall. We took
Each fence for a prophecy to be
Fulfilled, into whose heart we galloped
Through the hallooing and cursing, the booming hooves,
The inferno of gasping and snorting, the bright silk flashing.

Then the breathless rocking
Over the cruel ditch,
My fists on the curving neck; then the tremor
Of landing, the massive head flung back,
And the surging under my knees
For the next impossible hurdle.

II

With all affection dead, I learned their powers.
I raced with the hope of winning, not to win.
The young broke ribs and thighs, defiantly holding
To the old romance: great horse and gallant rider.

Older, the intense tragedians of one course too many,
They turned on themselves all season an unquenchable rage,
And drove their frothing horses until beast and man
Lay coupled in furious agony, thrashing the turf.

Once, launching easily over a laurel hedge,
I heard unearthly sobbing, loud;
Then the broken-back horse's scream
Before the steward's shot.

III

To learn that power, I surrendered
All claim to manhood. At the starting-gate,
I would bend my head to that place
Behind the ear, where the snout
Of the merciful gun would press.

Listening for the starter's bell, eyes closed,
Murmuring to calm my horse, I would see,
Clear and familiar as dream, the course,
And, winning or losing, the way we would cover it.

As always at the edge,
The fearful edge of that vision,
The others, their blurred colours:
Crimson, vermilion, gold.

IV

I became a single sinew
Cleft to the galloping animal.
Once, three fences from home,
I pulled up just in time
On a gelding of Amaryllis'
Bloodline. But, winning or losing,
No horse I rode could fall.

LESSONS

Your hand at my nape: the whirlwind
Rounds to close me in its circle.

Turn, and I am there,
A pillar of dust, a wind-worn
Pillar of limestone, casting
A rigid shadow over the yellow desert.

Were I to lift your hair
From your shoulders, the wind
Would sigh through far tamaracks.

You have taught me this touch, that gesture.
A snowdrop nods in first light.
Dawn prints your name on the hills.
Now, child, teach me to sing.

THE CONFESSION

To the grey rock below the silent park, in grey light,
The tide in its patient blind labour at last has yielded
The girl's white form. Her rigid nakedness

No longer could drive her lover to this murder,
Nor excite the youth who, finding her stretched there, is stiff
And cold with an unearthly fear, having discovered,

Once and for all, woman's mystery. With his coat
He has covered the trite flesh—a Shrovetide effigy
Cast into the sea at midnight when sinners turn

Penitent. In the condominium nearby,
Shadows are wavering behind the venetian blinds;
Roused early from their beds by the forlorn

Siren, a few emerge on their verandahs,
In bathrobes, hugging themselves, watching through opera-glasses
While a doctor kneels to hold her wrist, shaking

His head, and the sky stealthily brightens. The detective
Is staring at the sea, having pulled the boy's coat away.
They can see the black pubis on the wretched white

Branched form, and shivering, vanish inside.
Her lover regards his hands as though another's
Clenched and unclenched before him, remembering

The low sound in her throat when her body opened
For love. He will never make the detective understand
How, cherishing her every breath, he surrendered
All that torment and desire to the quiet waves.

IDENTIKIT

This is the one who did it all:
Medium build, neither short nor tall;
Eyebrows neither thick nor thin—
This is the one who'll do us in.

This is the one who got away
In a black sedan—a Chevrolet
Or a Ford—we can't be perfectly sure.
But this is the one, we're ready to swear.

This is the one with the evil nature.
No distinguishing scar or feature.
Eyes of an indeterminate hue.
This is the one, we're telling you.

You've got the picture, you can tell
From the face he's the mind of a criminal.
Johnny get your gun get your gun get your gun
This is the one. This is the one.

REFUGEES

Karkov the conjurer told the story at last,
On the journey over the plain to our final encampment,
Where we were to wait for the governor's verdict.
His thin frame jolted with the wagon; his grey eyes fixed
On our grey dust drifting over the dry, flat land.

I

"She'd been a baroness, then a refugee,
A figure of fun, her thin mouth set, politely
Smiling, the tendons drawn tight in her throat.
The frayed expensive frock, the stinking furs,
Were all she'd escaped with. A drunken infantry captain
Had raped her when the enemy commandeered
Her mansion. She told us of this, complaining
As if he'd merely slighted her at a banquet.

"For weeks she would not speak our peasant language,
But asked in French, with a courteous gesture of hands,
What she could do for the food we shared. I confess
I was awed by this woman"—his theatrical shrug,
His ironic mask—"and could not bring myself
To show her the mean tasks waiting everywhere
Around our camp—the stitching and scrubbing.
Hauling and cooking—every woman's lot.

II

"Ringmaster Albrecht, harsh and loud as ever,
Gave her to me in mock-marriage one night
After my act, in that town by the river-crossing.
A good crowd, much laughter, coins thrown at our feet."
Karkov shifted, his eyes steady on the dust
Pluming behind us in the fading light.

"She behaved as if our patched tent, reeking of dung,
Were the palace chapel—her slender arm extended
To accept the wire ring Zelf the clown had made;
Then sweeping on my arm through applause and laughter
While Felix coaxed a fanfare from his trumpet."
Karkov made tinny raspings through cupped hands.

"Wept like any bride in my bed, and kissed me,
And treated me like a champion those last few weeks,
As she must have treated the Baron, whom she'd seen
Shot down on the steps of their mansion, so she told me,
As he strode at the enemy captain with a horsewhip.

III

"Albrecht: you know he's crafty. And like us all,
He's superstitious. To preserve our luck
In a good season, we'd play the same province over,
His ring-master's coat-tails flying down muddy streets—
'Tonight! By popular demand! Repeat performance!''
Albrecht's brazen baritone in Karkov's throat.
The wagon rocked deliriously over the highway.
Grey eyes gleamed like wet stones in the gathering dark.
"And so, he announced our return to the town she'd fled.

"A rowdy crowd that evening, mostly soldiers
With schoolgirls, all drunk on raw spirits, all
Shrieking and roaring, making the animals nervous,
Distracting the high-wire girl with lewd catcalls.
The captain sat flushed in the front row, rolling
A cigar between his fine white teeth, very bored.
She was caging our two doves when she sighted him.

"Growling like a panther she crossed the ring and was on him,
Straddling him, gouging, snarling, rutting and rutting
Against his belted paunch. He could not break
Her terrible embrace—that thin frame all steel—
Till with a loud cry she spent against him. He threw
Her back then with great force, and she sprawled
In the sawdust and dung, cackling hideously.
Half-blind, raked from ear to ear by her claws,
He stood over her and emptied his pistol—" His grey eyes
Steady on the grey dust that pursued us.

25

LOSING THE WAY

I can tell from the map where I am.
All the highways and by-ways are marked;
Every village and town has its name.

By obeying these signs I can tame,
As I ride it, the sullen dark.
I can tell from the map where I am.

I know where to turn when I come
To a crossing: it's sure to be marked.
Many crossings embrace well-known names.

When I study it first, I can dream
The terrain as I go in the dark.
I can see from the map where I am.

But these journeys are never the same:
Places I seek are not marked,
And the streets are confused, with strange names.

When blind alleys break off in the dark,
And cartographers artfully mark
Dead-end streets, but accord them no names—
Who could tell from the map where I am?

PERSISTENCE

for Robin Skelton, Aet. L

Sloth lounges at our table, the fat shade
Of Falstaff, wickedly entertaining bounder,
Always so candid, logical. Friendships founder
In the rough seas of our despicable trade—
Our homes in disarray, our hopes delayed,
Yet the Bitch Muse duns us for a more resounding
Line, no sooner delivered than she's hounding
Us for its match, and the account is never paid.

We know how the story ends, but a cold delight
Keeps us aloof from our own part in the play
While we balance, for a figure, the soul's weight
Against the fleshed word, no better than spittle and clay,
In the Scales of Contradiction. Then we're the butt
Of Death's old joke again, and the devil to pay.

MAKING AN IMPRESSION

Graphite bruises the page.
Character by character, the slow
Pencil figures out my name.

The ballpoint riding over the paper in a rage
Makes no distinction between *Above* and *Below*.
To this one, profane and sacred are all the same.

The fountain-pen purses its lips, discreet,
Giving every appearance of taking me at my word.

The typewriter chews the poem with blackened teeth,
Chatting between bites, making absurd

Mistakes. The eraser wags a stubby finger at the neat
Unalterable lines I started with, now blurred.

TO HIS HOST, WHO HAS ASKED HIM TO STAY LONGER

We've learned in hard ways when we have to go.
There's nothing to explain, no one to blame,
And so much still to learn of love and sorrow.
Our children leave the house before their time,
Without a quarrel, casual, taking with them
Nothing to prize, and we may never know
What names they'll give their children. Nothing to do
But keep the house as neat as a chapel nave,
Lust after our friends' wives, let the wine flow,
Dance to old records, whooping like Indian braves.

We're lively enough, God knows, till the first one leaves.
It's a new kind of politeness we've let grow,
Going home when the party's in full swing to save
Our oldest friends the shame of letting it show,
This waking weariness that lays us all so low.
Tortured in our own beds by a hopeless fury,
We harp on how in youth we were always merry,
But can't remember now what made us so

AN IRISH BULL

(An incongruous mixture of metaphors, often humorous,
sometimes elusive or surreal, usually rendered in a political
context; a low species of oratory, developed during the
notorious filibusters of Parnell's party during the 1880's.)

for James Whitehead, Aet. XL

Political passion is the poorest coin
We trade with. Slumped at the screen like resigned
Brokers or navigators, we're the last,
We pretend, with the power to lend any value to words
So debased in the common exchange we feel them break
From their moorings in meaning when we bring them to meet

In metaphor—as if we could still make ends meet
Or tame any beast by such means. Words are coins
Thrown on a table to settle a debt, a sign
That nothing's settled.
                    In the news at last,
Franco is dead. The smart men give us the word:
"He was good for Spain." Then a commercial break.

Old Farrell, my countryman, twenty at the outbreak
Of that war when we both were born, went south to meet
A fascist slug that sent him home lame. No coin,
Spanish or Irish, could straighten his step, resigned
As he was in his hatred, his only hope to outlast
Those fanatical, bickering, stomachy men, whose word

Is good for Business, always a good word
With upstarts and fascists.
                              We've worked hard to break
Their code, to invest in a language that's meet;
But meanwhile the enemy we know has coined
A new name for himself, and left no sign
That's the least inimical; no word that lasts.

Rage in Belfast, Beirut, L.A. The last
News item, Dow-Jones bullish; then a word
From our sponsor. The doldrums, without a break
In sight. In the boredom of bad news we meet
Our worst enemy.
                        Better to toss a coin,
Tails for the fascists, sure to come up, and resign

Ourselves like Farrell to a bitterness designed
For our own good to bankrupt the spirit. The last
Word for them from the newsman leaves no word
Unturned: *conservative*. Euphemisms break
Into spume to show us where the breakers meet
The rocks we've sailed too close to.
                                            But if the coin

Turns up the imperious head of coins, could we assign
Politics a lasting language, find the exact words?
Or when the beast breaks loose, turn back to meet it?

TIMEPIECE

Needle and groove replay
A song I learned before
All songs became the same.
Something to rot the core
Is winding its way in.

Stripping, I leave my clothes
And watch, as if they bore
A grudge against my skin.
Something to rot the core
Is ticking its way in.

It's not easy to wake up.
I'm bent double, with the floor
Shaking between my feet.
Something rotten at the core
Is eating its way out.

The headlines don't amaze.
You can tell who's in power:
They leave you in no doubt.
Something rotten at the core
Is eating its way out.

My friends have sent a card
With its false view of the shore,
The sea, the sky. They write:
Something rotten at the core
Is eating its way out.

DEPOSITION OF HAROLD MOORE, GARDENER, AT THE INQUEST OF THE HON. MISS GLORIA MADELINE HASTINGS.

21st April, MCMXXXVI

I

The topiaries were just my pastime.
It amused me to clip those evergreens
Into the shapes of begging
Dogs or crowing cocks,
During slack times. She praised me
For those fancies, some said follies;
But she hardly noticed the trellis
Of climbing hybrid roses
Outside her study window,
That gave me so much trouble
Before the right yellow, dark
As gold, took the graft. I named
That one plant for her: Madeline.

Her whim was the croquet lawn:
Tiresome work, on my knees
Over every inch weeding out
Dandelion, clover, scutch-grass;
Then the roller every day
For weeks to get it as flat
As a table. I kept it that way
For years, though used but once.

At first there was plenty to do,
The limes in the drive to rescue
From a fungus, the walks to rake,
The banks of perennials
To thin out and make neat.
And when there was time, I tried
New hybrids in the hothouse,
Or clipped those green creatures.

II

She gave me a free hand,
Never a word of the cost,
Nor of praise either, when she strolled
Through the grounds in fine weather,
Stooping over her cane.
When she saw the Cupid
And the peacock and unicorn
I cut from the hedge between
The hothouse and the old stable,
She had to ask me my name
Before she could remark on them.

She sold the parkland for taxes
When the new government took over,
And paid off the indoor staff,
But kept me on. A day's work
Was enough by then to take care
Of what remained—lawn and gardens
Between the house and the road—
For half a season; though she seldom
Walked those paths any more.
I learned a new trade by taking

The bricks from the ruined stable
To wall out the sold land. On her side,
I planted a thick thorn hedge,
And let it grow wild.

Next, she had to sell
The lodge, where I'd lived from the day
She hired me. I moved to a room
In kitchen quarters; she taught me
To cook plain meals. We never
Ate together. Evenings,
She made me read to her.
I stumbled often at first
Over the strange words.

The house now stood among others,
Elm and birch cut down,
Replaced by bungalows,
On the land she had given up.
From behind the four wild hedges,
We heard the shouting children,
The weekend hammers and mowers.

III

We were reading *Vanity Fair*.
I thought she'd fallen asleep,
As she often did, both bony hands
Grasping the ebony cane,
While we sat there in her study.
I stayed watching her
Till first light surprised me.

I made a coffin of maple
Boards I raised from the old
Ballroom floor where no one had danced
For as long as I'd been there.
Then I made her a grave,
Not deep, on the croquet lawn.
I was in her service
One week short of thirty years.

I learned a seventh skill
By carving her name on the hearthstone
I hauled from the house to the lawn.
Just her name, and the year she died.
I knew none of the other details.

THE EXILE TAKES STOCK OF HIS SURROUNDINGS

We know who we are from the names
Engraved on the mail-order napkin rings.
We've been extinct for generations,
But our souls live on in the bargains
We hauled home from the discount stores.
(One lemon has to go back:
The stereo—a pretty white cube
From Woolworth—makes Sibelius
Sound like tugboats in fog.)
The old slope-shouldered fridge,
The motor clucking like barnfowl,
Was a steal at forty bucks
And a beer apiece to the gaping
Sophomores who delivered it.

Who will deliver us
From the food the kids won't eat
The hotdogs bloody with ketchup
Frenchfries like huge nailparings
We should deliver the rest
Of the Minute Rice to Dacca
Who will deliver us
From the empties stacked in the carport
From the lamp that shorted and burned
When we plugged it in (*antique*,
The woman meant: *extinct*,
I heard her say, *Five
Seventy-five as is* but took
Two bits off for good will).

Who will deliver us
From the blotched leaves on the plant
Dying in the window
Of the living-room behind
The yard-sale recliner
Still exuding disinfectant
And dead bugs on the rug
We bought from the Salvation Army—
Oh Lord, when they delivered
The secondhand king-size bed
That we couldn't resist or afford—
Deliver us, deliver us
From the junkmail trumpetings
Of white sales, bargains, bargains!

Our neighbour delivers the children
Home from nursery school.
They fall asleep over dinner.
The pork'n'beans grow cold.
The TV glows blue-green
On their faces. (A good buy
At twenty-five bucks from Abilities
Unlimited—works fine.)

DEATH OF FATHERS

for Ken McCullough

His plane exploded
In oily black and red
On the Persian desert:
The dusty crescent of mountains
Wheeling at the edge of vision;
The tawny ground veering up.

I felt it behind other dreams,
Waking up sweating and shaking,
To stare at myself while I shaved,
Slow to focus on my own face.

Every detail severely familiar:
The instruments warping and cracking,
The roar of flames in the cockpit;
His stern frown, one arm raised
To see better, unbelieving;
The ground reeling through the windshield.

What reason have I to believe
He died as he wanted to?

My mother took to the madhouse;
His mistress knelt discreetly
At the back of the church for the service
My uncles, my brother, and I
Brought the coffin with ashes
Gathered from the desert
To the family grave. It was all
Acted out with the proper restraint.

I'm cold enough now to let
This elegy rise between us.
All that time, every detail
Has stayed as clear as a curlew's
Call in the night: he still
Grips the useless controls;
The unchanged ground spins up.

OWEN AT PLAY

Owen from nothing imagines, then contrives,
A world where he's the sole intelligence.
Out of Tinkertoy parts, inert on the bedroom floor,
He re-enacts a galaxy's mighty fusion.
In his own good time, these reeling spiky suns
Will implode into characters—one-eyed, roundfaced, good
And bad—shoved about all their puny lives by huge
Incomprehensible grubby hands. All they know
Of their purpose in his design is a furious chiding
Wafted down to them on some celestial sheriff's
Seething breath. From him, mere clumsiness
Can earn a decapitation, or a season of doom;
Or, when he's in merciful mood, oblivion.

That whisper's a portent: whom he would destroy,
He renders helpless first with many small
Anxieties. Then anguish and terror spread
Indiscriminate through the frail universe.
Behold, not one bright block on another! Lo,
The *Realpolitik* of the animal circus! Weep
For the finger-puppet's plight, who's crammed
In a jig-saw box, the pieces long dispersed
Like holocaust atoms, heaven only knows where!

Wouldn't the Mother of God herself cry out
To him to cease and desist from this wrathful harvest?
Rest, inscrutable lawgiver, from your labours!
Postpone the Apocalypse; instead, bestow
On the chaos only you perceive order in,
Your sabbatical grace, the holy peace of your sleep!

41

THE PICTURE OF LITTLE RORY IN A MUNICIPAL PARK
Saxe Point, Victoria, B.C., January 1975

Rory, tired, dawdles on the path
Beneath the cedars where the light is dim,
As in ancestral caves. A bramble tugs
His sleeve.
          His chilled face, pale in the green shade,
Flanked by shards of fern, embraced by thorns—
Unlikely alabaster cherub in the profuse
Wilderness of a Douanier Rousseau—
No more my child than anyone's.
                  Behind him,
A massive boulder looms, the tumbled head
Of a crude colossus, hewn by the torpid ice
A million years ago.
           I've turned, intending
To hurry him up; but again I'm in the wrong
Place for fathers, under these boughs reduced
To a superfluous attendant.
              Now the light
Is fading quickly, threatening more snow;
And I've lost perspective.
            Rory, motionless
This moment in the whispering palace of cedars,
Is untimely pensive, as Velasquez made
His Infanta in the scene where dog and dwarf,
Maids of honour, the artist himself, are all
Stopped by a premonition in a room
As dark as the grove we're halted in.
               I'll call
Across this little distance, and he'll come
Slow as ice, footprint in melting snow
Small as a bird's, and beg to be carried home.

REQUIEM

in memory of my mother

I *Mourners*

The widow returns to the house
And accepts the quiet room,
The polished furniture.
Her hands rest in her lap.
She will soon find something to do
With her hands again. She says
His name aloud in the room.

*

The one whose shoulder aches
From the weight of his sister's coffin
Has turned his back to the wind
To light a cigarette.
Flame hollows his skull; wind
Rips the smoke from his hands.

*

The man whose wife is lying
Between the four tall candles
Waits for the women to leave,
Then climbs the stairs again
To quench the candles, one
By one. Then he sits all night
In the dark room beside her.

43

For the grieving are as numerous as the blades
Of the long reeds that bend in every wind,
Surviving, though their hollow roots hold sand.
As sorrow leaves us, so wind dies in the reeds.

II   *"Alle Herrlichkeit des Menschen"*

God of my childhood
Set free these dead
From the chains of my prayers.

God of the light
That fixes this dead
Shadow to my heel,

Make me in wisdom
Set free these dead
At last from my grief.

III   *Vigil*

In my town the old sea-captain
Whose skin was sailcloth, whose speech
Was a gusty spittle, whose lies
Were crimson anemones swaying
In the blue rockpools that ringed
The green edge of my town—

In my town the captain was last
From his wrecked ship in a roaring
November storm—the breeches buoy
Lifting him like a saint

Assumed into heaven over
The gnashing of rocks and sea
To the room with dim prints of ships
In full sail, where his pipe
Wheezed as he told me great lies.

In my town, at the rosary
The night they coffined him,
He was a wheyfaced pensioner
Already gone straight to heaven
With the reek of plug tobacco
For a halo. I'd never seen
Him before with his eyes closed.

IV *Glory*

I sifted the coarse yellow sand
Through the hollow of my fist.
My heels dug inches in sand.
I bit on a reed from the dune
Where our loving had left its mark.
I tasted its salt; I made
Coarse music with it, rasping
The corncrake's misleading call.

The girl with me held wide
Her towel to show me her dark
Nipples, her silky dark pubis,
And covered herself again quickly.
Her laughter and my cry
Of shame and delight were flung
Like seed on the calm bay.

Oh, survivors, who among you
Will grieve with me for those voices
Dying away in the whispering
Of small waves, the piping of birds?

V   Survivors

Chaplain

Four shells on four yards
Of trench in the stripped wood
The Somme, July 1916
O horrible, most horrible
Trapped him in a dugout
With three fusiliers who cursed
Their bad luck first, but prayed
With him later, panting,
Their words flat, hissing
On poisoned air.

The next barrage tore bright
Strips from their eyes: the sky
Opened over the foul trench.
In gaseous day, in the childish whining
Of unseen wounded, they joked
About his hair, turned white
In that four hours' burial.

After the hospital morphine,
They sent him to teach boys
Mathematics and History
Far behind the lines.
They let him grow dahlias and banks

Of rhododendrons in
The rich soil of the school grounds.
The boys called him *Thatch* or *Shakes*
Behind his back; but they liked it
When he took them to help in his garden.

Bombardier

The youth who took
An ack-ack shard
Below the ribs
Was so fixed on
His bombsight that
He felt only a slight
Loosening

Till the plane kicked up
Banking for home
And he leaned away
From the silver threads
Of the railyard in
The crosshairs

BOMBS AWAY he
Yelled reaching
For a cigarette.
Into the bowels
That filled his flight
Jacket he
Laughed and called
To the navigator
LOOK but the other
Was already dead

They sewed him back
Together but never
Could answer him
About his old buddy
His navigator

Skipper

A cable winching boxes
Of mackerel out of the hold
Snapped and tore both thighs.
In the Harbour Bar he drank
From their bottle of pre-war cognac
While he waited for the doctor.
Before he passed out, he sold
The trawler to his brother
For half its worth, and sent
A note up to the house
On the back of a factor's docket:
God has laid his curse
Now I am half a man.

In a black November storm
His brother ran the trawler
On Shenick Island, the rocks
Tearing the hull like new bread.

His brother was lost: the others
Brought off on the lifeboat safe
While he shouted the lost one's name
Into the flying spume, the luminous waves.

48

For everywhere in their places are heroes who dare
To carry their grief as Achilles bore his shield,
With Patrocles lost, into the maddening war.
Sorrow is with them everywhere, the shadow at the heel.

VI   *Creed*

The rocks here, if they sang,
Would chant *Affirm! Affirm!*
They pile down from the cliff,
A great choir petrified
In the act of singing the canticle's
Sublime chord: *Amen!*

From the clifftop a summer forest
Spreads a green infinity
To meet the infinite blue
Of the sky that commands: *Affirm!*

But the cell that set my hand
To trembling while I wrote
Lets go, and dies. I wait
For the shadow of the cliff
To bury the spilled rocks.

Then, having for this scene
Invented the dying sun,
I kneel in the wild grass
With nothing to deny.

49

VII *Labour and Tribulation*

Flattening dough for pastry,
Thumping the high kitchen table,
My mother's forearms swelled like a bosun's.
She hummed the musichall lovesongs
Of her girlhood—"Love's Old Sweet Song"
And "The Long, Long Road A-Winding"—
Every surface, all odours charmed
To attend her rare good humour.

Her hair was white at thirty.
My aunt (her advisor, though younger,
And pretty, and always in trouble
Over men) would sit with her drinking
A bottle of Powers between them
On wet Sunday afternoons
Worrying about money.
Their voices would bring me from reading
To the room where they changed the subject.

Soon from her hospital bed
She was scolding me: *Mind yourself.*
In north-city slang, we joked
About family misfortunes;
But she couldn't laugh as she used to,
Rocked by a giddy croaking—
One lung and most of the other
Gone; the family disease.

And soon after that we fought
Over money and didn't speak
For years; then I wrote
From America, signing

My childhood nickname. And soon
She was dead from too much whiskey
And pills and time on her hands
To worry about money, and about
Her thankless children, I suppose.

God of light and shadow
Let her rest in my understanding.

VIII   *Secret*

First light paints
The old shadow over
This familiar ceiling.

In childhood, I could make out
Satan's wing on the cracked
Plaster above my bed.

And rising, I would venture
Into the world of loss:
In the corner of my father's
Garden, a row of tender
Seedlings, the first from my hand,
Killed by late frost.

Such rising into cold light!
Such blind hammering
Barefisted on withered stalks
In the cracked crust of soil!

51

God of this new day
Set me free in your light
From such vain grief.

IX   *Blessing*

I will walk today
Accepting that shadow
For company

I will walk today
Treading dry leaves
Into the dry grass

I will walk today
With my children
In the wintry park

I will let them play till they tire.
I will grieve with them
Over their slightest loss.

THE EXILE CONSIDERS
HOW HIS LIFE IS SPENT

I claim the booze has killed the memory cells.
Late in the afternoon, I get down to answering letters,
But only because it's raining—otherwise,
I'd have gone to play golf, or study waterfowl
In the wildlife refuge through the binoculars.

Soon I give up on the letters and take to the couch.
Blocked in the empty house, with every blank
Sheet of paper shouting "DUTY!"—I close my eyes.
A neighbour pug barks shrilly; a robin warbles.
Is this Yoga? Let every muscle relax.
To begin, go rigid; then the instep, ankle, eyelid....

On the retinae, an expanse of plateau spreads
With rock and sagebrush far to the horizon
Where buttes thrust up into uncertain weather,
Streaks of cloud like mucus over the sky.

Into this uneasy prospect, the astute
Little Ohio storekeeper, on his way north
To the Yukon, halts his wagon to mend
A wheel. His journey's not for gold
Or thrills: he wants to give a settlement
The permanence of a town with hardware, dry goods....

His campfire's mirrored in a fissure of cold
Run-off from a distant glacier. Space
At sunrise radiates from him, intimating
The afterlife. What will he decide?

Routine, routine. Time to pick up the boys
From the kindergarten, buy a paper, get gas.
For all I know, he stayed at the river-crossing
He forded next day, still in Oregon Territory.
He might have fashioned a town, not much to his liking,
His expectations shrivelling, mean houses soon

Boarded up by the immigrants' children, who learned
To think, *This place is Hell.* Lights stop me a block
From the school. I figure it all out: his grizzled head
Crushed by an axehandle for the till's few dollars;
Blood streaming from him into the pale green river

As he trembles down through the rapids. Awake at 3 a.m.,
I feel those pickled cells the way an amputee
Aches in the emptiness under his elbow. Was this a story
Some cadging wino told me in an Idaho bar?
Which life is invented? Which episodes demonstrate

How the willed life is fruitless, or the converse?
If I say there's no wildlife refuge, iridescent wing
Curving up and back as it rises from water,
Does this cancel the robin's song, the murdered man?
What of the river, and the glaciated plateau?

MY UGLY FRIEND

His pocked skin stretches like old Swiss cheese
Over Slavic cheekbones that give him a squint.
He lurches across the room, one great paw
Reaching to greet me. His eyes pop and roll
Like a stunned bullock's: this is smiling. A squawk
Sputters between front teeth arranged like the blades
Of a plow. His handshake is sticky. "Hi, there!"
Is all he has uttered. I thought he had gasped his last.

"How've you been?" I reply. Stupid. It's clear
The poor guy could have nothing but bad times.
He licks thick lips and launches on a story
While I'm thinking of his life, the dreary apartment,
The take-home food, the nights of TV and Coke,
The bug-eyed gaping round the café for a place,
The church's pot-luck suppers where everyone's kind.

I tune back in while he's telling of this hot divorcée
Who's spending the weekend at his A-frame in the woods.
In the buff, they eat Swedish pancakes with sour cream.
Poor sonofabitch, a full rich fantasy life
Does wonders when Nature's dealt you a lousy hand....
I chuckle, to show him I'm with him all the way.

He's fetched, meanwhile, an iota of snot from his nose
And inspects it absently on his fingertip
While he explains that although she was great in bed
And a saint with a casserole, she wanted to re-marry—
Suburbia, kids, the whole bit—so he dumped her.

To put him at ease, I report how my last affair
Had also gone sour. He brays and slaps his knees
Like a gorilla. This is laughter. "Goddam,"
He wheezes, bug-eyed, "You're a lot like me!"

GOING LATE TO BED

I

Going late to bed, I heard the owl.
When I kissed your sleeping head, you groaned,
But did not wake. What sound bodes ill or well
At this low time, when body anchors mind
In desire's rip-tide?
"Who chooses?" quoth Owl from his clearing.
Here begins the tedious parade
Of hooting ghosts. Alarums. Broken moorings.

Now the trumpeting freight attacks the crossing
Six blocks away, the phantom engineer
Chanting to his pistons. Another lesson
Completes its Doppler curve with a clear "Beware!"

II

Another lesson the owl's chestnut eye.
It blinks, slow, stiff, a brown gem
Deep in the grove's green retina,
Where green slime in a phosphorous pool
Quakes like breathing flesh.
A vole makes a dry stirring
Under a dead tree in the close dark.

III

Fleshtint stagelight.
Enter draped figure,
Owlspeckled, mouthing.
Who chooses? Choose!

57

She raises a slender arm.
It grows encrusted, a dead
Branch in a thicket.

I enter crabwise,
Throat taut to groan
Or growl. I approach her
While this other eye watches,
Groaning. Exit.

IV

Enter through ludicrous
Chorus of peasantry
Swaying in unison
Round the wishingwell
At centre stage
The plaintive tenor
Advancing to footlights
Out of tune swaying
In pantaloons
Mouth caved arms branched
With a high note on "Beware!"

Alarums. Exeunt all, Owl mocking.

LOWER CASE

thank you cummings for this most amazing
method which next to of course god and the pretty
how of clabbered grammar gives a great de
flation to high matters and a mar
vellous flavour to the poe poe poets ideo
syncrasies popping up from dropping all the punc
tuation where its most expectorant

how well they understood your imitators
about suffering never suffering but suffering
their meagre tropes to come unto the page
measuring out their lays in fifths of rye
without ole EGOs caps to give the game
away with a lazy i
though could be
like ME
they find it hard to con
centrate upon
the keys for SHIFT and , and ; and my sweet old .

AFTER YEATS, AFTER RONSARD, *PACE* HOPKINS

When we've been divorced for a while, and you get
Edvard Münch postcards from the Netherlands,
And late-night calls to check whether we're still friends
(Your eyes closed, your changed lips ruefully set

Against forgiveness; yet lending a canny ear),
You'll recall my forecast: how these walls
Will hiss their own surly silence, when what galls
Is neither my presence nor absence. Ah, my dear,

You'll finally come looking for me, checking the bars;
I'll be easy to find; you'll curse me, but I'll pay
No attention, thinking *She's old and grey*.
So, bend now by this glowing fire, and thank your stars!

DIRECTIONS

You've got to understand
The central character
Is Philip. How would it play
If every time he gets home
From one of his big scenes
Your Miss Albright there
Rides his ass about
Not giving her a good time?
Eh? In the script she's the sweet
Type who never questions
Her lot, you understand?
      Yeah, but she wants to act,
      Well, *ironic*, you know?
      She lets everyone out there know
      She has this thing for the neighbour
      And while Philip's away on the job
      Fixing deals for his boss
      She's not just ironing his shorts—
Look, the script says nothing
About ironic.
There's no money in the budget
For ironic.
We'll shoot the scene tomorrow
Without ironic.
Philip tries to convince
Old Hart the mayor, the way
His boss has it figured, they can save
The town and cover up
The scandal with his daughter.
Understand? No ironic.

But Miss Albright—the wife, I mean—
Has to know of the scandal! You see?
She's in the big scene at the country club
When the cops arrive to pick up
Old Hart's daughter for questioning.
See what I mean about irony?
Miss Albright could ask Philip questions—
The wife, I mean—like "How's
Old Hart's girl holding up?"
You get it? Everyone out there
In Movieland would know of course
He's not just her lawyer—the daughter,
I mean—and anyway Philip—
Listen: we'll be rolling
Tomorrow with Old Hart
And Philip on the staircase
At the Hart place outside town.
The idea is he's welching
On his boss, he's too ambitious.
Philip, I mean. Your girl's part—
Miss Albright—is small, but *good*.
She's a clean straight woman who's wronged
By a husband gone to the bad.
It's a strong script—we don't need
Ironic, understand?

TAKE UP THY BED

(John, V.)

I

My earliest memory? Why, the lassitude!
The impatient servant's spoon at my mouth,
The long staring at the crude maps of my feet,
The cutting reek of urine, the dung-reek
Of my own bed—the scratching together of my thighs
When they carried me through the city to the waters.

My father in his prime died of the plague,
Howling his soul's curse at the marble walls.
They tell me his name is in the history-books
For his land reforms after the wars. At seventeen,
I inherited the cursed villa, and the green balm
Of the gardens, and his salaaming servants; and his fortune.
The sickness by then had drawn skin tight to bone.
The odour of a cow's belly cut open, of spewed offal
Rose about me wherever I lolled, while I dreamt
The indolent movement of others swaying about me.

My servants feared the spirit of my father;
So, for a decade, until they began to forget
His power, they carried me to the stinking baths—
What a figure I must have cut in my silk swaddlings,
My quaking head full of ideas, impressions,
The satin pillow wearing the hair from the nape,
My features a child's leathern mask for the game
Of "Beggars"—what a spectacle at the baths,
My Egyptians holding me naked in the bubbling mire!

And afterward, free for a while from my own stench,
I could lie in the garden, steeped in a cloud of birdsong;
Or bursting a grape on my palate with my tongue,
Numbness on numbness, yet the sweet grape bursting
While I had Old Lares recount a tale of men
On horseback, gripping sword and shield, doing battle
While the Emperor and his lovely Princess bore witness.
The clamour and brilliance of events could be as strong
For the brain as the burst grape on my tongue.

II

But Lares with the rest forgot in time
My father's spirit pacing the echoing rooms.
I woke one morning, sunlight full on my bed,
So bright that the painted figures on the walls,
The plump daemonic dancers, seemed to cavort
Alive in the ritual grove. Silence: The air waited
To tremble into piping, into the lewd drumming
Of bare feet on bare earth. My four senses
Tortured me with this silence. They had fled
At last, had stolen every trinket my father
Had hoarded. What fear must have travelled with them!
Why had they waited so long? And yet, how timely!

Three silent days. Then a gang of diseased slaves,
Turned out by their masters, crept through the villa like spiders.
They found me swathed in lambswool and satin. I pleaded
With them for days, till they bore me down to the baths
Where I could beg for scraps and dwell with others
Like me, stinking carcasses. Do they still haunt
My father's villa, worshipping frenzied gods? Or
Are the red-faced Roman captains quartered there?

III

A child of ten, no more,
Stuffed hard crusts in my mouth,
Her eyes fixed on my tongue
Choking down the rough crumbs.
Straw for a bed, like an animal;
A long dying, before the miracle.

IV

To feel at my heels the smooth stones,
The slime on the walls, the oily waters
Breaking brown on my brown skin—how strange!
The coarse cloth between my fingers, the scabs
On old sores, the dizzy business of standing—
Strange! Pain still clambers along this tree
Of nerves that grows from my heels into the old
Head, nodding queerly with the body's news—

Tongue clatters its new consonants
Like grapes bursting on my teeth. I hold
Another in my arms as I was held,
And ease him into the pool, learning patience.
How soon my whole being grows into its movements!

THE EXILE, *EN FAMILLE*

Among my own, I'm a figure of fun,
A bare-fanged clown, even in anger.
When I'm half-asleep over a book
Of literary criticism, or consumed
By passions that last a week for eating apples
Or gluing models or pruning plum-trees—in
My clumsiness, untidiness, my untimely
Trade, my distractedness, they mock
Generously. I've learned to pay them
No mind. Without contempt, my children
Ignore my commands, my rules for safety first,
Tuning their nerves to a frequency
That transmits but won't receive.
But that's all right: for their part,
They burden me with tasks so trivial,
Oiling a hinge, fixing a window, tying
A shoelace, while my head is filled
With keeping a ketch's bow into the wind,
Or listening to Brahms and Tolstoy talking
While they stroll a riverbank—I accomplish
Their love at small cost. As the trout
Leaping from the pool in the willow shade
Needs the deadly air to remind him
Of his element, and would not forego
The glistening arch he carves—
So, while I bend to repair
The broken window, I remember:
I accomplish their love at small cost.

IMPROMPTU FOR SOLO TENOR

Daniel O'Connell could address a crowd
Of half-a-million with his own raw voice,
No microphone. Lapsed Catholics talk softly,
Passionately, of loss. In the confessional,
The penitent whispers to the priest who sits
Up straight on his side of the screen, whispering.

Sisters speak one word with all their feelings
Rifled at each other. My only brother,
When he talks, blames me and forgives
With his eyes. I understand. Also the woman
Who talks to me only with her small hand
At rest on her thigh: I hear you!

NATURAL HISTORY
a nocturne, for Helga Heinrich.

The curlew is not extinct.
Wolfgang, who works with doves
At the Göttingen Institute,
Told us so after dinner,
Whistling their mating-call
By way of reassurance:

A long rising note, then short piping,
Not shrill; six fluted notes.

The fluttering quick coitus.
The hen patient on the nest,
The eggs casual as pebbles;
The bald young all leathery mouthing.

The wild sound in his living-room
Has left us wordless. Here
In the tidy patchwork of beetfields
Near Göttingen and the cruel
Border "between Germany and Germany",
We're far from their salt habitat,
Where they are not extinct.

Their delicate trident tracks
Writ in sand at Barnageera,
Where they probed the sand with long beaks,
Rising in a cloud on wings

Of sand, wings of salt, when my dog
Charged, barking, frantic over
The wet corrugations at low tide,
Those long afternoons
Before the blackberry season.

The frail egg melted
Into a monster, blotched,
Wingless with mercury
Poisoning. Their mating-call
Is on tape at the Institute:
The curlew is not extinct.

When the weather blew down from the north
At blackberry season's close,
They would gather in the dark
Above our house: one high note
And its echo, like a question.

Perils of the lighthouse beam,
Storms off the Atlantic . . . .
Their resting-places now
Landfill, refineries, summer villas.

Their high crying bodiless,
Fading downwind, downwind,
To Biscay, Samothrace.
The tide creeps over their tracks
In the sand at Barnageera.
The curlew is not extinct.

THE OLD WRITER

talks over a pale wet underlip,
an endless, fleshy admonition
couched as memory: *Never grow
this old*—and pats his pockets
for a handkerchief, wheezing
gleefully about hard cash,
keeping his distance between dead friends.

A woman in her fifties, big eyes
of a tawny owl, a turtle's mouth,
is constant at his shoulder, one
pace exactly behind him, watching
everything. The pendant of pearly snot
in his moustache is one thing she can do
nothing about, till later in the hotel
she will humiliate him—*You
looked so foolish!*—through the bathroom door.

* * *

Old writers should not accept invitations.
Simple questions excite them, as
How long did you know Joyce in Zürich? Or,
*Didn't you live with that girl Aetna while
you wrote your second book?* Now too old
to dissemble, he answers to his companion's
dismay, *Yes, she could sing too we got along
famously and Jim you know still owes
me ninety franks would cross the bridge*

into the Dörfli near the art museum
where we had a room she didn't like
Jim when he got drunk but we had good times
till she went to Milan that season to sing in "Norma"—

He warbles wetly. The watchful woman
laughs harshly and helps him into his coat,
then steers him back to the hotel. Her grip
on his arm is a painful signal: *Quiet!*
She'll soon correct his memory
concerning the girl Aetna, whom he'd loved
when Turtlemouth was a pigtail wretch: *Writers*,
she'll say, *should never grow this old!*

ASTRONOMY

These nerves, these nebulae,
Filter a thin light
Years in all directions;
All cluttered creation looms.
God, anonymous as frost,
Relaxes over seven
Dissolving galaxies.

My head, this wrinkled planet,
Keeps emitting a garbled message.
Cells die, dissolve, in the other
Galaxies—Abdomen, Wrist,
Larynx, Aorta, Eyelid,
And lonely, remote little Penis.
God stretches, yawns, turns His back.
Black holes drink the stars where He was.

WAR CRIMINAL

Nothing I could say would answer you.
Legion upon legion of my kind,
Marched into court, tried, hanged, and buried
In quicklime, would still leave you ravenous.
The others from those trials in the newsreels,
So long ago, with their little sleepless smiles—
Their shame was yours too, who doled out guilt
Like fruit or cigarettes. And if you were right,
Look what trouble I've gone to, removing the past,
All the past. And you have taken—how long?—
Thirty years and more to find me here.
I can give you nothing for your records.
This name you give me, I will deny to the end.

At the plant, I had a friend who told me
His war story, drinking all afternoon
Watching football in a bar on Franklin Street.
He served in Italy, he said: an easy time
Herding old men and boys to prison camps.
We laughed together—his story was so good
For him, he didn't ask for mine. He too
Confessed nothing; but he could tell of looting,
Of a prisoner set on fire, of a shorn woman.
You understand, there are so many victims
And witnesses: what need is there for me
To confess anything? You make me a gift of guilt.

No: you are strangers; and I'm too old for hate.
Besides, of those years you insist on, that place,
I can picture only harvest-time, the ripe
Wheatfields sloping up to green woods,
The pale light, the smooth silvery trunk of a beech-tree.
And you above all, with your sense of duty, of mission,
When you are certain your long hunt is over,
What will be your reward? Will you start a new life?
Will you wake from nightmares, whispering *Innocent?*

Details? Details? I will deny such details!
Yes, let these survivors confront me—
What will they see? A pensioner with arthritis,
Who walks his stupid old dog by the river, drinks
With the other old men in the bar downtown,
Small-talk and pretzels, beef jerky and football games;
Twenty-five years a machinist at the plant,
Look, photos of my marriage, she was a nurse,
Older than me, dead three years, our son
A forester in Colorado with two children,
They came for a day to visit me last Fall—
What could they find in me after thirty years
To remind them of such details, these survivors?

CONCLUSIONS

for Liz Cook

I've been too long in this place.
The worst ideas sit
In the best chairs, like old men
In nursing-homes, kept alive
Against their will. Time to pack
And move. But I have so much
Baggage.... Shame
Sits at the edge of the bed,
Cracking knuckles. To take
Nothing with me, just stand
Up and walk out, clean,
With only my hands in my pockets;
Not so much as a toothpick
Or a rosary. See how far I can go,
Clean, sound, when I want to. Despair
Leans back on the pillow, eyes closed.

SUCCUBUS

Phantom senses waken where you lie.
But it begins in oblivion, the truth
You could tell later—not in the form she takes
While now you feel her hand caressing you.

Twisting from her, you find her name with your tongue.
Listening to her humming, learning the air,
You come to like that music well enough.

The chords you feel vibrating under your hand,
The song you hear, the woman you embrace,
Her voice calling your name, though she's no more
Than the warm air constricting you like a sheet—

These you will assume in the story, told
Later, ephemeral as your own quick breath
Haunting the dark, giving you the lie

Already, while you can remember the name
She gave you, and the trembling instrument
She made of you, so you could learn by heart
A mystery. Now, bloodless, she recedes.

FOR THE THREE SONS OF MY FIRST MARRIAGE

Jim, Tony, Kevin
> *". . . For I am weary of considerations"*—Robt. Frost

Consider the science of origins: how cells
Divide into trinities of dying—
Their sundering from one shape to another,
As these lines break under my hand
Into a small chorus, a lifetime of murmurs.

Unbridled from your childhood, taking what wrongs
And grace you care to carry with you
On memory's iron frame, consider these
Cells ridding themselves of you, their calm sonata,
As on a May evening, when birdsong has failed

For want of light, an old song rises to darkness,
Lines battening on absence—you and I
By nature not acquainted with much else.
Limpets on shipwreck change the iron shape
Of what we know to blunt guess and silence.

Consider freedom, the blind fit we wrench from,
As a cormorant, a flapping tombstone, scarcely
Able to lift from water, yet trusts in flight!
So I am free from this clumsy distance to bless you
Calmly, knowing what trinity of pain

Stretches between us from the time I began
Leaving, before the invention of old
Songs you have learned by heart through all their changes.
I can join in their chorus, a lifetime of murmurs
Surrendering to silence, like evening birdsong.

MORALITY PLAY

I

This girl, nineteen, adjusts,
Slightly, her blouse. Small breasts;
Her features unremarkable,
Unlined. Her fair locks parted
Straight down her scalp, surely
By divine decree. She
Believes, I can tell.
        And—not for long—I dwell
On how, with her mother's wiles
Packed tight in her brain's coils,
She'd still not find much wrong
With my hand unbuttoning
This ludricous cheap blouse,
Sky-blue, with little clouds
Of darker forget-me-nots.
        But after love, there'd be lots
Of mooning and babytalk;
Later, her scolding, the salt
For endless silent resentment.
It's all written there, relentless
Across the flat bust, the bare
Scalp where she's parted her hair
At the severe mirror—the lot!—
Make-up and blouse—not a jot
Or a tittle awry, all these hard
Hours.
        At the window, I regard
The foundered ribs of snow
On the pale grass, lying low;
On my scalp, a crown of soft pain.

II

      Teaching such girls is a strain;
In every encounter, they train
To be tightlipped mothers, spouses.
For these comrades-in-buttoned-blouses,
The Supreme Commander is Jesus:
Nothing's changed since the Middle Ages.
      Her features are as plain as the Bible
I'd be perjured on if I libelled
Her in a fanciful trial
Of her virtue. I'd certainly fail,
If I wooed—God Forbid!—and won,
And lived with her in sin
Till Doomsday's trump, to taint
Her neat soul. For this complaint,
There's no lawbook to give me due
Process.
      A boy in blue
Winter coat and jeans picks her up
After class, ungainly pup!

III

      The sky has had this raw grain,
Like the underside of the brain,
For weeks. Walking home, I feel
Insensate: the Unreal
Is my guide through a labyrinth,
As though I had drunk of absinthe . . . .
      Cares abound. But I'll be tame,
And turn enough cheek to hum
Aloud through my teeth to the trees
Clamped in frost; no ease
Could I teach *them*, for any season.
I hum like these pines: I have reason!

79

THE ARTIST, RECLINING

She leans forward; he is lying exhausted
After their making love. His head, at ease
In her lap, is careless and quiet for once,
The star fixed in a clear sky, waiting
        For its name.

When he turns his head to kiss her breast,
Her heartbeat rises to his lips, the language
For a whole history of art: Renoir,
Brush fastened to his wrist, would make
Her lean forward like this, and then describe
With easy, luminous strokes, his gratitude
        For the making.

FLOOD

We lost the reach of time
In the wrong season for this weather. The rain
Beat a tambourine
Over the roof, and gulleyed down innumerable channels—
Was it four or five days
Before we quit counting? We watched, amazed,
The antique process through our liquid windows,
Drawn from the idleness enforced
By the spectacle itself—all that silvery light,
And the black ground hardly withstanding!

Now this night, it set
A new pitch that roused us from shallow sleep,
Impelling us to begin
Lifting utensils and keepsakes from their places.
With that odd cheer
Our kind brings to disaster, we tried to reckon
How long, and what power in water would rise
Against us. Soon we learned,
Simply by listening, not by calculation,
That our choices had run out.

We started uphill.
Our flashlights made spangled strings of rain
Like a fortune-teller's curtain
Through which we carried boxes of books and papers,
The radio, the model ship
From over the mantel—we set it all in a pile
Under the torn tarpaulin on the hilltop
And assured ourselves by their disorder we'd soon
Return them to their places in the house.

81

We huddled in our oilskins.
Quited by cold, anxious for day, I dropped
Into a blank stupor.
Tittering finches woke me. The rain had stopped.
Light spilled slowly
Like thick yellow cream from the east behind me
Over the scene for which we were prepared,
Yet were confounded by.

More like a harrowed field you could walk across
From ridge to ridge, brown as our best topsoil,
Except where the poor light
Spun out on its surface—there,
You could mark how fast it moved, a stump
Waltzing round and round with a dead beast,
A mailbox tumbling
In a carousel of chattels—I choked back a laugh—
The cab of our pickup
Was inching solemnly down the rumbling torrent!

The alarm-clock started its prattling under the tarp,
Advising us to rise
For a day's work. No one had the heart
To stifle it. By noon,
The waters were holding level under the dormer
That stared ruefully from the house at our drenched camp.

That afternoon, we heard
A highpitched rasping south behind the trees,
And Fred, our mailman, steered
His old aluminum punt aslant the current,
Calm as Vergil in Hell,
To give us passage to the school where half
The town had taken shelter. As for the others,

82

Some survived—the stubborn, the drunk, the defiant—
Fred told us. He had seen
Their ghostly faces in attic windows. Some folks,
He explained, possessed too much to be saved.

The week had to end
In a gold relenting clarity of air
Before the waters eased
Back between the old banks, a river again,
Though keeping a sullen brown;
Then we stood knee-deep in sucking mire
Like a living creature in our kitchen.
We girded ourselves to begin again,
Mouthing to each other the old sayings—
"Lucky to be alive"—as charms against
Despair; and replaced
On mantel and shelf our paltry mementos.

DROUGHT

The phone sits on the wall, a starved insect.
I could call you anywhere on the globe,
It's me, Jim—chewed into thin whining strips
Of wire and wind and spittle. Nine hours sooner
Or later you'd choke down a tinny capsule
Of sound, don't you remember? *It's me, it's me!*
My hand unfolds from the phone, a stricken insect.

This is no occasion for a letter,
Except I have forgiven myself in time
For the dead I didn't write to. The seasons here
Effect so little change that when the lake
At Coeur d'Alene is lowest in memory,
It's surely worth my mentioning. Besides,
You can easily find that lake on any globe,

Even so small a scale; and it's close to where
I live. All through these parts the drought gains ground.
Our neighbours, who at the best of times are silent,
Now are fervidly dumb. Good luck is the thin
Stalk in the flowerpatch that held the head
Of the pale aster for a week, then let go.
You could be dead, and I would still write this letter.

HOUSE BURNING DOWN

What fire feeds on is mostly air, but I dwell
On what I own, how bitterly I'd start over.
Flame leafs through a shelf of books in minutes:
The pages swell to rippling levels of yellow.

Hoses curl from the engines to the men
Who lean away from the seething jets, the glare
On their faces like saints beholding a vision.

The busy lapping inside that unfixed roar
Holds to a staunch pattern. I draw closer
Through my fear—if only I could command
Fire, the oldest language—those feral labials!

Now books and shelf are one. Flame sheaths the roofbeam.
To a great shout of timbers, the house leans inward.
The doorway conjures a seamless yellow curtain
Over the vanishing rooms. Fire smiles in the teeth
Of a cellar window, then pours up a firmament of sparks.

Flames chatter to each other, a fierce lingo.
I turn my back to recall the names of objects
Liquified by flame: *book, lamp, table, chair.*

And on my way home I call a blessing
On every sleeping house against the black
From which the yellow flame will soon depart.

IN PASSING

Here, all sorrow ends.
Tell me your life story
And I'll tell mine, though I'd rather
Lie. But, this once, why bother?
We've both been here before,
On the thin line between friends.

What have we concealed
From each other? At the window,
Bare branches spell in code
Something we've left unsaid.
But we've taken leave of sorrow.
This way, our lips are sealed.

Your eyes examine the walls
As if I'd written there
The makeshift words I've used
To keep you here, amused
At my prattle, my white hair.
What danger could you tell

From what I didn't say?
You start from me like a plover
With her false wound from the nest
We both know can't exist.
I want to be your lover:
My last lame word is *Stay*.

All sorrow ends in this.
November's here, to be sure.
The wind plays at Cassandra
In the bare trees. Who understands her?
The word unsaid is *Fear*.
Would you leave with a hurried kiss?

IDOLATRY

Humbled before each other, priestess and priest
Giddy with ritual, leaving our clothes, we feel
The world turn turtle. Naked, we are the pale
Children of winter nibbling at a feast
Of small pains. Last year's sun has traced
A dark curve over your heart. We blaze a trail
Of little ceremonies, till we come to seal
A covenant that could make smooth the least
Tremor at the edge of your mouth.

                          You dress,
Your skirt dancing about you, and I catch
My breath on your perfume. Still, when we kiss
Solemnly at leave-taking, I watch
Your amber eyes cloud with a small distress,
As if you felt on your breast the sun's touch.

HABITATIONS

I

Burnt pine etches pungency;
The fire's gone down.
With the house to myself like this,
And the room beginning to chill,
I can feel the plateau rising
Under the snow to high peaks
Between here and the Pacific.

The record is back in its sheath,
The melody from Brahms
Lingering, hesitating.
If I exhale, it is gone,
Like a radio signal fading
Over great distance. Already,

Outside, a long sound has filled
The expanse of air between
Blue moonlit snow and sky:
The coyote's sheer keening,
The high vowels of loss.

II

In this trance before sleep,
I am nineteen again;
I have just switched off
The late-night jazz from Holland.
A lorry on the hill
Outside the Santry house
I'd never cared to live in
Grinds its gears, hauling hay
To market in Dublin.

On those nights, road sounds
And the blast of plane engines
Revving in maintenance hangars
At the airport would lend
That house its only substance.

III

Mother, sisters, brother,
Sleep tonight in the memory
Of those rooms, the frayed rugs,
The scarred mahogany furniture,
The hallstand mirror filling
With the ghosts of passing headlights.

One sister's hair is spread
On the pillow like a mermaid's
In the tide; the other sighs
Like an opera heroine;
My brother, even in sleep,
Wears his anxious frown.

My mother is lying awake:
My father is absent again,
His Grumman on the oily
Orinoco roaring
Out for take-off.

*

The stairs creak with my weight;
As always, I'm last to bed.

RECITAL

There's a certain way to do this, right or wrong.
Crossing your legs can be a matter of taste.
Plenty of seats in front–but watch your tongue!

Who listens to a naked woman's song?
Playing Brahms or Verdi, do you feel chaste?
There are certain ways to do this, right or wrong.

The metronome, the tuning-fork's keen prong–
Nothing you do with passion is a waste.
Plenty of seats in front—but hold your tongue!

Don't assume your beloved knows how long
It has been since you first sat down and faced
The certain way to do this, right or wrong.

And Petrarch, in the chapel at Avignon:
Could he have seen Laura praying while she graced
The seat in front of him, and held *his* tongue?

There's plain water to drink at every feast,
And jewels adorn, whether real diamonds or paste.
How you feel is neither right or wrong;
Plenty of seats in front, if you hold your tongue!

WITHDRAWN FROM STOCK